THE ACROSTIC SUMMARIZED BIBLE

BARRY HUDDLESTON

BAKER BOOK HOUSE
Grand Rapids, Michigan 49516

ISBN: 0-8010-4351-4

Second printing, September 1992

Printed in the United States of America

Because of the unusual design requirements for this volume, several Old Testament books do not appear in the normal sequence. The books of Job and Esther have been reversed as have the books of Ezekiel and Lamentations. All other books—in both the Old and New Testaments—are in the proper order. The publisher regrets any inconvenience these changes may cause.

Library of Congress Cataloging-in-Publication Data

Huddleston, Barry.
    The acrostic summarized Bible.

    Includes index.
    1. Bible—Miscellanea. 2. Acrostics.
I. Title.
BS613.H68 242   78-2329
ISBN 0-8010-4351-4

INTRODUCTION

Acrostics are nothing new. They are as timeless as the pages of Scripture and as contemporary as the morning newspaper.

Even in Bible times acrostics were known and used. The Old Testament contains fourteen acrostic poems, the most notable being Psalm 119. Though there are no acrostics in the New Testament, the early Christians identified one another by drawing the sign of a fish—in the Greek *ichthus*—an acrostic for the Greek words meaning "Jesus Christ God's Son, Savior."

Chances are you use acrostics nearly every day of your life. Piano students often learn the lines of the treble clef with the aid of an acrostic: "*E*very *G*ood *B*oy *D*oes *F*ine"—EGBDF. Acrostics have rescued many a grocery shopper who has arranged the list of needed items in such a way as to spell an easily remembered word. For example, here is a list of seven items. Read it over, close your eyes, and then try to recall all seven:

Onions
Watermelon
Soup
Flour
Relish
Eggs
Lettuce

Now try again, this time with the aid of an acrostic. By rearranging these seven items into a particular order, you will find that their first letters spell the word FLOW-ERS. Now can you recall all seven?

In much the same way, Bible readers down through the centuries have sought ways to remember the contents of Scripture. Ever since Stephen Langton hit upon the idea of dividing the Bible into chapters in A.D. 1228, men have searched for newer and

better techniques for summarizing and memorizing God's inspired Word. What Sunday school teacher hasn't used the acrostic of GRACE (God's Riches At Christ's Expense) and FAITH (Forsaking All I Trust Him) to help the learning process?

You hold in your hands perhaps the most significant contribution yet to that continuing search. Barry Huddleston has created a unique approach that meets the three greatest needs of the serious Bible student: (1) a chapter-by-chapter summary of the Bible; (2) a thematic overview of each of the sixty-six books; and (3) a topical index that aids quick location of every chapter in the Bible dealing with a particular subject.

Barry's idea, encouraged in a class taught by Professor Terry Hall (a member of the Walk Thru the Bible Ministries team), is designed to provide the Christian with a synthetic, memorable tool for getting a "nuts and bolts" grasp of the Bible. It is simple, yet profound; exhaustive, yet memorable.

In *The Acrostic Bible,* short four-word phrases introduce each chapter of the Bible—from Genesis to Revelation. Then, reading down the page, the first letter of each chapter phrase forms another word, phrase, or sentence that accurately—yet succinctly—captures the theme of the book. The vocabulary is pungent and pithy, just right for implanting itself deep in the mind and staying there . . . perhaps for a lifetime.

As president of Walk Thru the Bible Ministries, an organization committed to teaching the Bible in a memorable and useful manner, I heartily commend *The Acrostic Bible* to you. My hope is that a perusal of *The Acrostic Bible* will become a standard "first step" in your personal Bible study. I challenge you to commit five minutes of the time you spend each day in God's Word to memorizing the chapter phrases in *The Acrostic Bible* for the book in the Bible you are studying. It will introduce you to the contents of the book and help you retain far more of the truth you will encounter.

When you have transplanted into your mind and heart the descriptive chapter phrases and book themes from the pages of *The Acrostic Bible,* then you will be ready to study and absorb the contents of that book of the Bible—verse by verse.

Bruce H. Wilkinson
Walk Thru the Bible Ministries
Atlanta, Georgia

THE
ACROSTIC
SUMMARIZED
BIBLE

GENESIS

1 Inception of the world
2 Newlyweds placed in Eden

3 Temptation and man's fall
4 Hatred and first murder
5 Entire genealogy of Adam

6 Building of the ark
7 Eruption of the flood
8 Going from the ark
9 Initiation of rainbow promise
10 Noah's sons and grandsons
11 Nations scattered from Babel
12 Immigration of Abram's family
13 Nephew Lot leaves Abram
14 Gifts for Priest Melchizedek

15 God counts Abram righteous
16 Offspring Ishmael from Hagar
17 Designation changed to Abraham

18 Compassion for Sodom's righteous
19 Removal of Sodom, Gomorrah
20 Egyptian escapade of Abraham
21 Arrival of promised Isaac
22 Test of Abraham's faith
23 End of Sarah's life
24 Denoting Rebekah as bride

25 Twins Esau, Jacob born
26 Hostility between Isaac, Philistines
27 Esau robbed of birthright

28 **H**eavenly ladder at Bethel
29 **E**arning Leah and Rachel
30 **A**dditions to Jacob's family
31 **V**enture away from Laban
32 **E**ndeavoring to wrestle God
33 **N**ew friendship with Esau

34 **A**venge for Dinah's defilement
35 **N**ame changed to Israel
36 **D**escendants of Esau listed

37 **T**reachery of Joseph's brothers
38 **H**arlot Tamar deceives Judah
39 **E**nraged Potiphar jails Joseph

40 **E**xplanation of two dreams
41 **A**ppointing Joseph as ruler
42 **R**euben held in Egypt
43 **T**rek to Egypt again
44 **H**olding Benjamin for cup

45 **A**nnouncement of Joseph's identity
46 **N**ew home in Egypt
47 **D**esign to save Egypt

48 **M**anasseh and Ephraim adopted
49 **A**nnouncement of Jacob's blessing
50 **N**ew relationship among brothers

EXODUS

1 **F**orced labor for Israel
2 **R**oyal training for Moses
3 **O**bstinate Moses resists God
4 **M**oses' excuses are answered

5 **E**gyptian oppression is increased
6 **G**od's deliverance is promised
7 **Y**ahweh smites the Nile
8 **P**lagues of frogs, insects
9 **T**hree plagues harden Pharaoh
10 **S**warming locusts and darkness

11 **B**lood required for firstborn
12 **O**bservance of the Passover
13 **N**ational exodus from Egypt
14 **D**ivision of Red Sea
15 **A**doration song to God
16 **G**athering manna six days
17 **E**xtracting water from rock

18 **T**ribal organization for ruling
19 **O**rders at Mount Sinai

20 **S**tatement of Ten Commandments
21 **I**njunctions for moral justice
22 **N**umerous laws of restitution
23 **A**ngelic assistance is promised
24 **I**nstructing Moses on Sinai
25 **S**ketch of tabernacle plans

26 **T**abernacle curtains and boards
27 **E**xact measurements for tabernacle
28 **N**ecessary garments for priests

29 **C**onsecrations of the priests
30 **O**fferings for sin's atonement
31 **M**andate to keep Sabbath
32 **M**olten calf brings judgment
33 **A**nguished intercession by Moses
34 **N**ew covenant is given
35 **D**esire rekindled for tabernacle
36 **M**aking curtains and boards
37 **E**xplanation of furniture making
38 **N**ew court for tabernacle
39 **T**abernacle and garments finished
40 **S**hekinah glory fills tabernacle

LEVITICUS

1 **H**oliness demands burnt offerings
2 **A**cceptance of meal offerings
3 **N**ecessity of peace offerings
4 **D**emand for sin offering
5 **B**urnt offerings for trespasses
6 **O**ffering laws for priests
7 **O**ffering laws for priests
8 **K**eeping the priest consecrated

9 **O**ffering of Aaron's sacrifice
10 **F**ire consumes Nadab, Abihu

11 **W**arning against unclean animals
12 **O**fferings for birth purification
13 **R**equirements for unclean lepers
14 **S**ign of cleansing lepers
15 **H**ygiene for human uncleanness
16 **I**nstitution of annual atonement
17 **P**rominence of the blood

18 **F**orbidding of sexual impurities
19 **O**rders to be holy
20 **R**estrictions against moral sin

NUMBERS

1 Tallying Israel by tribes
2 Host organized for marching
3 Exchanging Levites for firstborn

4 Work of the Levites
5 Instructions for judging adulterers
6 Law of the Nazirites
7 Description of leaders' offerings
8 Emphasis on Levitical cleansing
9 Record of second Passover
10 Nation leaves Mount Sinai
11 Elders and quails given
12 Sin of Miriam's murmuring
13 Spies sent from Kadesh-barnea

14 Judgment on Israel's unbelief
15 Offerings for the land
16 Uprising led by Korah
17 Rod of Aaron buds
18 Necessity of priestly service
19 Eleazar and red heifer
20 Years of wandering end

21 Overthrow of the Amorites
22 Fear of Balaam's donkey

DEUTERONOMY

1 **R**etelling of Israel's failures
2 **E**nd of Israel's wanderings
3 **P**ossessing Gilead and Bashan
4 **E**xhortation to obey God
5 **A**pplying the Ten Commandments
6 **T**eaching children the law
7 **I**dolatry to be destroyed
8 **N**ecessity of God's testing
9 **G**od's grace after intercession

10 **T**ablets for the ark
11 **H**eritage for obeying God
12 **E**xhortation to holy separation

13 **L**ying prophets must die
14 **A**nimals suitable for eating
15 **W**ay of remitting debts

16 **F**easts listed and explained
17 **O**bliteration of all evildoers
18 **R**ights of the Levites

19 **I**nvoluntary killer given refuge
20 **S**trategy for God's warfare
21 **R**ights of captive women
22 **A**dultery and morality laws
23 **E**xclusions from the assemblies
24 **L**eaving a mate legally
25 **S**ummary of civil laws

26 **O**ffering of firstfruits
27 **B**uilding the Ebal altar
28 **E**xtended blessings and cursings
29 **D**isobedience will bring curses
30 **I**nitiative for following God
31 **E**stablishment of Joshua's leading
32 **N**ew song of Moses
33 **C**onferring the tribal blessings
34 **E**nd of Moses' life

JOSHUA

1 **P**rosperity promised for obedience
2 **R**ahab protects two spies
3 **O**nward through the Jordan
4 **M**emorial stones are set
5 **I**srael's circumcision at Gilgal
6 **S**uccessful conquest of Jericho
7 **E**nd of Achan's coveting
8 **D**efeat of Ai's army

9 **L**ying by the Gibeonites
10 **A**ttack of five kings
11 **N**orthern kings are conquered
12 **D**iary of defeated kings

13 **M**ethod of land division
14 **E**xpectations of Caleb rewarded
15 **A**pportionment to Judah's sons
16 **N**iche for Ephraim tribe
17 **S**elfishness of Manasseh satisfied

18 **V**ictory proclaimed in Shiloh
19 **I**nheritance given to Joshua
20 **C**ities of refuge named
21 **T**owns of Levites named
22 **O**ffense of the altar
23 **R**ehearsing of the law
24 **Y**ears of Joshua end

JUDGES

1 **T**erritories Israel left unconquered
2 **H**ow God tested Israel
3 **E**hud slays Moab's king

4 **J**abin overcome by Deborah
5 **U**plifting song of Deborah
6 **D**etermination via Gideon's fleece
7 **G**ideon's army routs Midianites
8 **E**phod causes Gideon's downfall
9 **S**hechemites make Abimelech king

10 **O**ppression by the Ammonites
11 **F**ighting Jephthah subdues
Ammonites

12 **G**ileadites overcome the Ephraimites
13 **O**ppression by the Philistines
14 **D**eceit over Samson's riddle
15 **S**amson kills thousand Philistines

16 **P**hilistines find Samson's secret
17 **E**phraimite hires own priest
18 **O**ffenses committed by Danites
19 **P**erversion of Levite's concubine
20 **L**evite's vengeance on Benjamites
21 **E**xistence of Benjamin assured

DE JUDGE

RUTH

1 **R**uth returns with Naomi
2 **U**nlimited gleaning from Boaz
3 **T**ime for kinsman redeemer
4 **H**usband redeemer for Ruth

FIRST SAMUEL

1 **B**irth of Hannah's son
2 **I**mmorality of Eli's sons
3 **R**evelation of Eli's judgment
4 **T**ragedy of ark's capture
5 **H**eavenly glory leaves Israel

6 **O**fferings with returned ark
7 **F**oreign gods are removed

8 **S**tubborn request for king
9 **A**ppointment of Saul arranged
10 **M**aking Saul Israel's king
11 **U**nified defense of Jabesh
12 **E**xhortation against demanding king
13 **L**esson of Saul's foolishness

14 **T**riumph of Jonathan's attack

15 **H**opelessness of Saul's disobedience

16 **R**ecord of David's anointing

17 **O**verthrow of giant Goliath

18 **U**nfriendly Saul threatens David

19 **G**uarding David from Saul

20 **H**elpful Jonathan shields David

21 **D**avid demands priests' provisions

22 **A**himelech killed by Saul

23 **V**ictory over the Philistines

24 **I**ntegrity shown by David

25 **D**eath of Samuel mourned

26 **S**aul spared by David

27 **E**xile in Philistine territory

28 **X**-rated seance with witch

29 **I**ntegrity of David challenged

30 **L**oss of Ziklag avenged

31 **E**nd of Saul's life

SECOND SAMUEL

1 **H**eaviness of David's heart
2 **I**shbosheth made Israel's king
3 **S**adness over Abner's death
4 **T**orture of Ishbosheth's killers
5 **O**utset of David's reign
6 **R**emoving ark to Jerusalem
7 **Y**earning to build temple

8 **O**ppressors subdued by David
9 **F**avor shown to Mephibosheth

10 **T**riumph over Ammonite alliance
11 **H**ypocrisy of David's adultery
12 **E**ffects of David's sin

13 **R**eproach placed upon Tamar
14 **E**xiled Absalom comes home
15 **I**nsurrection by son Absalom
16 **G**ravity of Ahithophel's advice
17 **N**ature of Hushai's counsel

18 **O**pposition by Absalom ends
19 **F**orgiving of Absalom's followers

20 **D**eath of rebellious Sheba
21 **A**vengement on Saul's sons
22 **V**ictory psalm by David
23 **I**dentity of David's men
24 **D**avid's census brings plague

FIRST KINGS

1 **S**olomon anointed Israel's king
2 **O**pponents of David killed
3 **L**ord gives Solomon wisdom
4 **O**fficers of King Solomon
5 **M**aterials for temple requested
6 **O**uter temple is completed
7 **N**ature of Hiram's work

8 **S**olomon's prayer of dedication
9 **I**nstruction for Solomon's covenant
10 **N**ature of Solomon's riches
11 **S**olomon's wives bring idolatry

12 **I**nsurrection of northern tribes
13 **S**in of unnamed prophet
14 **R**eign of King Jeroboam
15 **A**bijam and Asa reign
16 **E**vildoers Omri and Ahab
17 **L**ord provides Elijah food

18 **S**overeignty shown on Carmel
19 **P**rophet Elijah calls Elisha
20 **L**oss by Syrian army
21 **I**njustice in Naboth's vineyard
22 **T**ermination of Ahab's life

SECOND KINGS

1 **K**ing Ahaziah is judged
2 **I**ntern Elisha receives mantle
3 **N**orthern kingdom conquers Moab
4 **G**ehazi and Elisha's miracles
5 **S**even dips restore Naaman

6 **A**rmy invisible but ready
7 **N**ews of Syrian departure
8 **D**ire predictions of Elisha

9 **C**ommissioning of King Jehu
10 **A**hab's seventy sons killed
11 **P**riest Jehoiada crowns Joash
12 **T**emple repairs are made
13 **I**ll Elisha prophesies victory
14 **V**ictory proclaimed over Judah
15 **I**dolatrous kings of Israel
16 **T**emple heathenized by Ahaz
17 **Y**ielding Israel to Assyria

18 **O**pposing Assyria by Hezekiah
19 **F**all of Assyrian army

20 **I**llness reversed for Hezekiah
21 **S**ins of Manasseh abound
22 **R**ecovery of God's law
23 **A**nnals of Josiah's purification
24 **E**xile of King Jehoiachin
25 **L**ast siege of Jerusalem

FIRST CHRONICLES

1 **D**escendants Adam to Edom
2 **E**ach descendant of Judah
3 **A**ll of David's sons
4 **T**ribes of Judah, Simeon
5 **H**ouses of Reuben, Gad

6 **O**ffspring of Levi's sons
7 **F**our sons of Issachar

8 **S**ons of Benjamin's tribe
9 **A**ssigned positions for Levites
10 **U**gly end of Saul
11 **L**eaders in David's army

12 **T**ribal totals of army
13 **H**and on ark disciplined
14 **R**aids of Philistines repelled
15 **O**btaining ark for Jerusalem
16 **U**nited celebration at tabernacle
17 **G**od's covenant with David
18 **H**armony through David's reign

19 **D**efeat of Ammon, Syria
20 **A**ssault against the Philistines
21 **V**erdict against David's census
22 **I**nstructions to build temple
23 **D**avid organizes Levitical duties
24 **S**ervices assigned temple priests

25 **R**esponsibilities of temple musicians
26 **E**mployment of gate keepers
27 **I**sraelite army division commanders
28 **G**uidelines for building temple
29 **N**ecessary materials given gladly

SECOND CHRONICLES

1 **R**equest for God's wisdom
2 **E**nlistment of Hiram's help
3 **I**nitiation of temple construction
4 **G**arnishments of the temple
5 **N**ew home for ark

6 **O**ffering temple dedication prayer
7 **F**illing temple with glory

8 **S**olomon's cities and sacrifices
9 **O**bservations by Sheba's queen
10 **L**eaders reject Rehoboam's harshness
11 **O**ffenses strengthened by Rehoboam
12 **M**istake of Rehoboam judged
13 **O**vercoming Israel under Abijah
14 **N**arrative of Asa's faith

15 **T**emporal reforms of Asa
16 **H**yprocrisy and Asa's death
17 **R**evival under King Jehoshaphat
18 **O**ffenses done by Jehoshaphat
19 **U**se of impartial judges
20 **G**od's victory over Moab
21 **H**orrible reign of Jehoram

EZRA

1 **T**emple proclamation by Cyrus
2 **E**xiles return under Zerubbabel
3 **M**aking the temple foundation
4 **P**ostponement of the work
5 **L**etter written to Darius
6 **E**xiles finish the temple

7 **W**arrant authorizing Ezra's return
8 **O**utline of Ezra's return
9 **R**epentance prayer by Ezra
10 **K**eeping foreign wives judged

NEHEMIAH

1 **J**erusalem's tragic plight mourned
2 **E**nlisting the king's support
3 **R**ecord of all workers
4 **U**ndermining attacks by Samaritans
5 **S**elling Jewish children renounced
6 **A**ssembling wall despite opposition
7 **L**edger of returning Jews
8 **E**xplanation of God's law
9 **M**aking confessions of sin

10 **W**itnesses to signed covenant
11 **A**ccount of Jerusalem's leaders
12 **L**evites lead temple dedication
13 **L**evites restored to temple

JOB

1 **J**ob's prosperity and tragedies
2 **O**utbreak against Job physically
3 **B**irth cursed by Job

4 **G**ather what is sown (Ez)
5 **O**rdinary case of chastening (Ez)
6 **D**enial of Eliphaz's charge (J)
7 **S**upplication against God's mistreatment (J)

8 **S**uffering befalls only wicked (B)
9 **U**nfortunate helplessness of man (J)
10 **F**airness of God questioned (J)
11 **F**inite man must repent (Z)
12 **E**vident truths animals know (J)
13 **R**esolution to debate God (J)
14 **I**nsignificance of man's destiny (J)
15 **N**ecessity of sin's punishment (Ez)
16 **G**od's affliction for innocence (J)

17 **S**alvation only in death (J)
18 **E**nd of wicked described (B)
19 **R**ehashing of God's mistreatment (J)
20 **V**engeance on wicked certain (Z)
21 **A**ntithesis of rich wicked (J)
22 **N**eglect of good deeds (Ez)
23 **T**ired of seeking God (J)

24 **I**nquisition on unpunished sin (J)
25 **S**ubmission of unjust men (B)

26 **T**ranscendence of God's greatness (J)
27 **E**vildoers' fate in life (J)
28 **S**ource of man's wisdom (J)
29 **T**riumphs of Job's past (J)
30 **E**xpression of Job's plight (J)
31 **D**enial of false charges (J)

32 **A**nalysis by young Elihu (Eu)
33 **N**ature of God's revelation (Eu)
34 **D**iscipline reason for trials (Eu)

35 **R**epudiation of Job's protests (Eu)
36 **E**xplanation of God's ways (Eu)
37 **S**overeignty of God's ways (Eu)
38 **T**ough questions on nature (G)
39 **O**rdinary animals show ignorance (G)
40 **R**evelation of Job's impotence (G)
41 **E**xample of leviathan's power (G)
42 **D**eliverance from Job's trials

Speakers: Eliphaz-Ez; Job-J; Bildad-B;
  Zophar-Z; Elihu-Eu; God-G

ESTHER

1 **P**ersian decree against Vashti
2 **U**ncle Mordecai saves king
3 **R**evenge plotted by Haman
4 **I**ntercession made to Esther
5 **M**aking dinner of Ahasuerus

6 **F**avor shown to Mordecai
7 **E**sther requests her life
8 **A**hasuerus gives Mordecai promotion
9 **S**ons of Haman hanged
10 **T**estimony to Mordecai's greatness

PSALMS

Praise psalms	9, 18, 21, 30, 47, 48, 63, 67, 71, 75, 84, 89, 92, 96, 99, 100, 103, 108, 111, 112, 113, 115, 116, 117, 124, 134, 135, 138, 145, 146, 147, 148, 149, 150
Remorse psalms	32, 38, 39, 51, 79, 85, 101, 130, 143
Acrostic psalms	119
Imprecatory psalms	10, 35, 52, 55, 56, 58, 59, 64, 69, 83, 109, 125, 129, 137, 140, 141, 144
Supplication psalms	3, 4, 6, 11, 12, 13, 20, 25, 26, 27, 28, 36, 42, 43, 54, 57, 60, 61, 70, 74, 80, 86, 88, 90, 120, 122, 123, 142
Environmental psalms	8, 19, 29, 33, 65, 93, 98, 104
Historical psalms	44, 66, 77, 78, 81, 95, 105, 106, 114, 132, 136
Instructional psalms	1, 5, 7, 14, 15, 17, 34, 37, 49, 50, 53, 62, 73, 76, 82, 87, 91, 94, 107, 121, 126, 127, 128, 131, 133, 139
Messianic psalms	2, 16, 22, 23, 24, 31, 40, 41, 45, 46, 68, 72, 97, 102, 110, 118

PROVERBS

1 Usefulness of God's wisdom
2 Nature of strange women
3 Discipline results in wisdom
4 Exhortation to get wisdom
5 Results of sinful lust
6 Sluggard, ant, strange women
7 Temptation by strange women
8 Appeal to God's wisdom
9 Necessity of God's wisdom
10 Diligence compared to slothfulness
11 Instructions for the righteous
12 Nature of the righteous
13 Good understanding produces favor

14 Applications for the wise
15 New use of tongue
16 Destruction of the proud

17 Unity of good friends
18 Safety through God's wisdom
19 Instruction on personal priorities
20 Nobility of trusting God
21 Governor of men's hearts

22 **G**ood reputation in life
23 **O**ffense of loving riches
24 **D**escription of evil men
25 **S**olomon's proverbs on humility

26 **W**ays of the fool
27 **I**llusion of man's wisdom
28 **S**enselessness of denying sin
29 **D**elights of godly wisdom
30 **O**racles given by Agur
31 **M**arks of virtuous woman

ECCLESIASTES

1 **E**mptiness of accumulating wealth
2 **C**onclusion to seeking pleasure
3 **C**ompleteness of God's timing
4 **L**abor is also vanity
5 **E**xhortations on hoarding wealth
6 **S**in is never satisfying
7 **I**nadequacy of being affluent
8 **A**buse of God's authority
9 **S**ame end for all
10 **T**emporary wisdom of man
11 **E**mptiness of godless living
12 **S**erving God brings satisfaction

SONG OF SOLOMON

1 **T**estimony of bride's love
2 **H**eart yearnings of bride
3 **E**xpectations of the bride
4 **B**ridegroom expresses his love
5 **R**esponse of the bride
6 **I**nterval when two separated
7 **D**esire expressed for intimacy
8 **E**xpectations of the bride

ISAIAH

1 **T**ruth of Israel's corruption
2 **H**opelessness of Israel's pride
3 **E**xecution of Judah's leaders

4 **P**urging sin from Jerusalem
5 **R**emoval of God's vineyard
6 **O**pening of Isaiah's lips
7 **P**rophecy of virgin's child
8 **H**orror of Assyrian invasion
9 **E**stablishing of Messiah's kingdom
10 **C**allousness of Assyrian army
11 **I**ntervention of Jesse's branch
12 **E**xalting the Lord's salvation
13 **S**ure destruction of Babylon

14 **O**verthrow of proud Lucifer
15 **F**ailure of Moab predicted

16 **I**nvasion of Moab's fall
17 **S**ins of Damascus exposed
18 **A**nnouncement of Ethiopia's doom
19 **I**niquities of Egypt judged
20 **A**ssyria takes Egyptians captive
21 **H**orrible vision of Babylon

22 **C**alamity in Jerusalem foretold
23 **O**racle given concerning Tyre
24 **N**ations judged by God
25 **C**ries of praise Godward
26 **E**xaltation of restored Israel
27 **R**estoration of God's people
28 **N**orthern kingdom is warned
29 **I**mpending discipline of Ariel
30 **N**o help from Egypt
31 **G**od's judgment of Egypt

32 **T**riumph of righteous king
33 **H**opeless future of Assyria
34 **E**nd of Edom predicted

35 **J**oyful shouting in Zion
36 **U**psetting news for Hezekiah
37 **D**oom comes to Sennacherib
38 **G**od grants Hezekiah's prayer
39 **M**essengers arrive from Babylon
40 **E**ternal comfort from God
41 **N**ature of God's power
42 **T**riumph of God's Servant

43 **A**ssurance of Israel's forgiveness
44 **N**onsense of serving idols
45 **D**eliverance by King Cyrus

46 **R**uin of Babylon's idols
47 **E**nd of Babylon's existence
48 **D**eliverance of Israel promised
49 **E**xpectation of God's Servant
50 **M**en responsible for sins
51 **P**atience of God's salvation
52 **T**orture of God's Servant
53 **I**ntercession of God's Servant
54 **O**ffer of God's compassion
55 **N**ecessity of seeking God

56 **O**bedience required by God
57 **F**alse leaders are rebuked

58 **J**ehovah's requirements for holiness
59 **E**vil blocks God's blessing
60 **R**isen glory of Zion
61 **U**nveiling of Messiah's work
62 **S**alvation promised to Zion
63 **A**ncient mercies are recalled
64 **L**ord's remnant gives thanks
65 **E**ternal heaven and earth
66 **M**essage of Zion's future

JEREMIAH

1 **P**rophet Jeremiah is called
2 **R**eview of Jerusalem's apostasy
3 **O**ffer of God's pardon
4 **P**rediction of Judah's ruin
5 **H**orror of Judah's punishment
6 **E**nemy conquers from north
7 **C**ounterfeit worship of God
8 **I**nsensitivity toward Judah's sin
9 **E**xile and ruin foretold
10 **S**enselessness of idol worship

11 **O**utcome of Judah's disobedience
12 **F**aithfulness of God's judgment

13 **J**eremiah hides linen girdle
14 **E**xhortation about coming drought
15 **R**epentance no longer option
16 **E**xile and return predicted
17 **M**isdirection of man's heart
18 **I**llustration from potter's house
19 **A**nnihilation of potter's vessel
20 **H**opelessness felt by Jeremiah

21 **O**verthrow of Jerusalem imminent
22 **N**ation of Judah warned

23 **T**rue and false shepherds
24 **H**earts return to God
25 **E**limination of lying prophets

26 **C**onspiracy to murder Jeremiah
27 **A**llegiance to king encouraged
28 **P**rophet Hananiah is judged
29 **T**ime of Israel's restoration
30 **I**srael's deliverance is promised
31 **V**oicing the new covenant
32 **I**nside prison Jeremiah prays
33 **T**hrone of David's Branch
34 **Y**ears of Zedekiah reviewed

35 **A**cceptance of the Rechabites
36 **N**ew scroll is written
37 **D**etention in the prison

38 **F**inal chance for Zedekiah
39 **A**nnouncement of Jerusalem's fall
40 **L**oyal Jeremiah remains behind
41 **L**owly crimes of Ishmael

42 **O**ffense of trusting Egypt
43 **F**light to Egypt wrong

44 **J**ews threatened in Egypt
45 **E**rror of Baruch's selfishness
46 **R**uin of Egypt foretold
47 **U**pset of Philistines foretold
48 **S**iege of Moab predicted
49 **A**ttacks on surrounding nations
50 **L**ofty Babylon will fall
51 **E**xtinction of Babylon foretold
52 **M**emorial of Jerusalem's fall

EZEKIEL

1 **T**hrone vision of Ezekiel
2 **H**earing of God's call
3 **E**ndowment of God's Spirit

4 **P**ortrayal of Jerusalem's judgment
5 **R**azor pictures Israel's punishment
6 **O**bliteration of high places
7 **P**owerless Israel against God
8 **H**orrible sins in temple
9 **E**xecution of Jerusalem's idolators
10 **C**herubim seen leaving temple
11 **I**dolatrous leaders are judged
12 **E**xile dramatized by Ezekiel
13 **S**tatement against false prophets

14 **O**rder to forsake idols
15 **F**ire to consume Jerusalem

16 **E**xamples of spiritual prostitution
17 **Z**edekiah rebels against Babylon
18 **E**ach person held responsible
19 **K**ing like trapped animal
20 **I**srael's history of rebellion
21 **E**xecutioner's sword over Jerusalem
22 **L**egal case against Jerusalem

23 **A**ssyrians and Babylonians coming
24 **B**oiling pot pictures judgment
25 **O**ther surrounding nations judged
26 **U**tter destruction of Tyre
27 **T**yre lamented for desolation

28 **J**udgment of king's pride
29 **E**gypt will become desolate
30 **R**uthless Babylon destroys Egypt
31 **U**ndoing of Pharaoh's pride
32 **S**laying of Pharaoh's army
33 **A**nnouncement of Jerusalem's fall
34 **L**ove of great shepherd
35 **E**xaltation over Edom's desolation
36 **M**iraculous restoration of Israel

37 **A**nnouncement of Israel's regather-
    ing
38 **N**ations allied with Gog
39 **D**estruction of Gog predicted

40 **T**emple courtyard is measured
41 **H**oly place is measured
42 **E**very chamber measured apart

43 **T**emple filled with glory
44 **E**xcluding some from temple
45 **M**andates regarding the prince
46 **P**rince's passageways and offerings
47 **L**and boundaries of Israel
48 **E**ach tribe given territory

LAMENTATIONS

1 **D**esolation of Jerusalem announced
2 **I**srael's misery is lamented
3 **R**eminder of God's mercy
4 **G**rimness of Israel's sin
5 **E**xiles pray for mercy

DANIEL

1 **D**aniel favored by Nebuchadnezzar
2 **A**nswer to king's dream
3 **N**ebuchadnezzar's furnace of fire
4 **I**nterpretation of tree vision
5 **E**vents at Belshazzar's feast
6 **L**ion's den of Darius
7 **S**cenes of coming kingdoms

8 **F**eatures of four beasts
9 **A**ppointing the seventy weeks
10 **I**nterpreting the final vision
11 **T**error of the king
12 **H**orror of end times

HOSEA

1 **G**omer's marriage and children
2 **O**ffenses of Gomer condemned
3 **M**essage of second marriage
4 **E**rror of Israel's ways
5 **R**ebuke of Israel's leaders

6 **T**estimony of God's love
7 **H**opelessness of Israel's desertion
8 **E**xile unavoidable for Israel

9 **H**arlotry will be punished
10 **A**ssyria will enslave Israel
11 **R**ebellion against God's love
12 **L**egal case against Israel
13 **O**verthrow of Ephraim certain
14 **T**ransformation if Israel repents

JOEL

1 **C**ry to avoid judgment
2 **R**eturn to God's blessing
3 **Y**ield to God's sovereignty

AMOS

1 **J**udgment on Judah's neighbors
2 **U**ngodliness of Israel explained
3 **D**estruction of Israel coming
4 **G**od's reproofs went unnoticed
5 **M**aking plea for repentance
6 **E**limination of unrighteous wealthy
7 **N**ature of God's judgments
8 **T**ime ripe for judgment
9 **S**cattering and Israel's restoration

OBADIAH

Verses
1–9   **E**dom's doom is prophesied
10–14   **S**ins of the Edomites
15–16   **A**ccountability of all nations
17–21   **U**ltimate restoration of Israel

JONAH

1 **F**light from God's presence
2 **I**ntercession from within fish
3 **S**ackcloth worn in Nineveh
4 **H**uman failure of Jonah

MICAH

1 **M**essages against Samaria, Jerusalem
2 **E**vils of Israel's people
3 **S**ins of Israel's leaders
4 **S**overeign king in Zion
5 **I**ntroduction of Bethlehem's Messiah
6 **A**ctions of injustice rebuked
7 **H**ope in God's future

NAHUM

1 **G**od's character and judgment
2 **O**verthrow of Nineveh imminent
3 **D**etails of Nineveh's judgment

HABAKKUK

1 **W**hy is evil unpunished
2 **H**aughty Chaldea will fall
3 **Y**ielding to God's sovereignty

ZEPHANIAH

1 **J**udah's day of wrath
2 **E**nemies of Judah punished
3 **W**rath and coming restoration

HAGGAI

1 **G**od's temple needs building
2 **O**lder temple less glorious

ZECHARIAH

1 **M**eaning of Zechariah's vision
2 **E**xamination with measuring line
3 **S**atan and the Branch
4 **S**even lampstands of gold
5 **I**nterpreting the flying scroll
6 **A**ct of crowning Joshua
7 **H**earts become like flint
8 **S**ecurity comes to Jerusalem

9 **R**eturn of the Messiah
10 **E**phraim and Judah restored
11 **T**eaching about wicked shepherds
12 **U**nderstanding whom they pierced
13 **R**efining of God's remnant
14 **N**ew kingdom ushered in

MALACHI

1 **L**ord reproves and reminds
2 **O**ffenses of the priests
3 **R**obbing God is cursed
4 **D**awning of new day

MATTHEW

1 **G**enealogy of Jesus Christ
2 **O**pposition of King Herod
3 **S**pirit's descent upon Jesus
4 **P**ower over Satan's temptations
5 **E**xpounding Sermon on Mount
6 **L**essons on proper priorities

7 **O**utline for personal relationships
8 **F**aith of the centurion

9 **M**atthew's call from Jesus
10 **A**postles sent to preach
11 **T**estimony about John's message
12 **T**rue Messiah called demonic
13 **H**idden message of parables
14 **E**xecution of John the baptist
15 **W**isdom in answering Pharisees

16 **K**eys of the kingdom
17 **I**mpact of Jesus' transfiguration
18 **N**eed for true forgiveness
19 **G**rounds for divorce clarified

20 **O**pportunities in the vineyard
21 **F**ig tree is cursed

22 **T**axes paid to Caesar
23 **H**ypocrisy denounced by "woes"
24 **E**vents of second coming

25 **J**udgment of the nations
26 **E**vents on Calvary's eve
27 **W**ay of the cross
28 **S**avior's resurrection and commission

MARK

1 **C**hrist the working Servant
2 **H**ealing of the paralytic
3 **R**esults of divided house
4 **I**llustration of the soils
5 **S**ervant's power over Gerasene
6 **T**eaching the five thousand

7 **T**raditions of Pharisees attacked
8 **H**ealing the blind man
9 **E**lijah at the transfiguration

10 **S**ervant attitude is mandatory
11 **E**ntry into Jerusalem triumphant
12 **R**esurrection queries are answered
13 **V**iolent destruction of temple
14 **A**gony experienced at Gethsemane
15 **N**arrative of Jesus' death
16 **T**omb is found empty

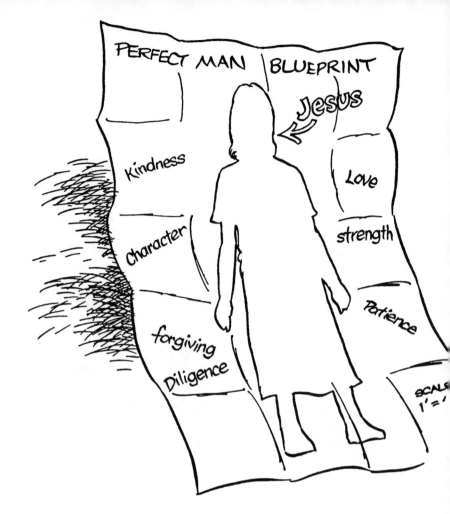

LUKE

1	**J**ohn named by Zacharias	12	**T**ruth of the Lord's return
2	**E**vents during Jesus' childhood	13	**H**ealing on the Sabbath
3	**S**pirit descends on Jesus	14	**E**mphasis on true discipleship
4	**U**ndergoing the tempter's tests		
5	**S**imon Peter follows Jesus	15	**P**rodigal son is received
		16	**E**ntrance into Abraham's bosom
6	**C**hoosing the twelve disciples	17	**R**esponse of ten lepers
7	**H**ealing the centurion's servant	18	**F**aith must be persistent
8	**R**ejection by the Gerasenes	19	**E**ntry into Jerusalem triumphant
9	**I**nstruction given on discipleship	20	**C**hrist repeatedly outwits Pharisees
10	**S**eventy preach and report	21	**T**emple destruction is foretold
11	**T**hundering woes against Pharisees		

JOHN

1 **J**esus is the Word
2 **O**utstanding miracle at Cana
3 **H**eavenly birth taught to Nicodemus
4 **N**eed of Samaritan woman

5 **T**estimony to Jesus' deity
6 **H**oly Bread of life
7 **E**xclamation at the feast

8 **G**race for adulteress defended
9 **O**pposition to removing blindness
10 **S**hepherd and His sheep
11 **P**ower to raise Lazarus
12 **E**ntry into Jerusalem triumphant
13 **L**ast supper and discourse

ACTS

1 **H**eavenly ascension of Christ
2 **O**utpouring of Holy Spirit
3 **L**ame man is healed
4 **Y**ield from public preaching

5 **S**apphira and Ananias judged
6 **P**roviding deacons ends injustice
7 **I**ntensive defense by Stephen
8 **R**ising persecution scatters church
9 **I**ntroducing Saul to gospel
10 **T**aking gospel to Cornelius

11 **W**orship with Gentiles defended
12 **O**utbreak from the prison
13 **R**elaying gospel to Antioch
14 **K**indness mixed with confusion
15 **I**nvestigation by Jerusalem Council
16 **N**eed for Timothy's circumcision
17 **G**ospel presentation in Athens

18 **I**nterview with Aquila, Priscilla
19 **N**ew believers in Ephesus

20 **T**ouching farewell from Ephesians
21 **H**oly Spirit warns Paul
22 **E**ffect of Paul's testimony

23 **C**ouncil of the Sanhedrin
24 **H**earing held by Felix
25 **U**rgent appeal to Caesar
26 **R**easoning with King Agrippa
27 **C**aesarea to Malta Island
28 **H**eralding gospel in chains

ROMANS

1 **T**estimony about man's sinfulness
2 **H**uman judgment of sin
3 **E**vidence of God's justification

4 **G**od counts Abraham righteous
5 **O**btaining righteousness by Christ
6 **S**inful nature is crucified
7 **P**roblem of continued sin
8 **E**xperiencing freedom in Christ
9 **L**ove shown for Israel

FIRST CORINTHIANS

1 **E**xhortation to Christian unity
2 **R**esponse of natural man
3 **R**easons for Christian carnality
4 **O**bservations on Paul's ministry
5 **R**ebuking immorality in church
6 **S**ins against the body

7 **I**nstructions for marriage partners
8 **N**ever be a stumbling block

9 **B**elievers must yield rights
10 **E**xpect victory over temptation
11 **H**ow to approach Communion
12 **A**bilities within Christ's body
13 **V**irtues of true love
14 **I**nstructions on using tongues
15 **O**rder in the resurrections
16 **R**eminders about spiritual helpers

SECOND CORINTHIANS

1 **T**estimony to Paul's sincerity
2 **H**eaviness of Paul's heart
3 **E**xcellence of the new covenant

4 **T**emporal versus eternal ministry
5 **R**econciliation offered to all
6 **U**nion with unbelievers forbidden
7 **E**xhortation to perfect holiness

8 **G**enerosity of the Macedonians
9 **O**pportunity for cheerful giving
10 **S**piritual authority of Paul
11 **P**aul's boastings in Christ
12 **E**xperience of Paul's thorn
13 **L**ives that stand the test

GALATIANS

1 **T**urning from true gospel
2 **H**ypocrisy found in Peter
3 **E**xample of Abraham's faith
4 **L**aw versus liberty
5 **A**ttitudes from Spirit's leading
6 **W**in back erring believers

EPHESIANS

1 **C**alling of the church
2 **H**eavenly position for individuals
3 **U**nderstanding of the mystery
4 **R**easons for spiritual gifts
5 **C**hrist's example for marriage
6 **H**elp in spiritual warfare

PHILIPPIANS

1 **J**oy of Christian fellowship
2 **O**utward evidences of humility
3 **Y**earning to know Christ
4 **S**ufficiency of God's provisions

COLOSSIANS

1 **H**ope produced by Christ
2 **O**bjections to false teachers
3 **P**rinciples for Christian life-style
4 **E**xpectant prayer and greetings

FIRST THESSALONIANS

1 **F**aith of Thessalonian church
2 **A**postolic labors in Thessalonica
3 **I**nvestigation of church's welfare
4 **T**rue love between Christians
5 **H**ope in Christ's return

SECOND THESSALONIANS

1 **D**escription of Thessalonians' faith
2 **A**postasy in last days
3 **Y**ield fruit through work

FIRST TIMOTHY

1 **A**dvice concerning false teachings
2 **D**irections for godly women
3 **V**irtues of Christian elders
4 **I**nstruction for godly living
5 **C**ounsel concerning the widows
6 **E**ffects of worldly living

SECOND TIMOTHY

1 **H**old on to true faith
2 **O**bey and teach the Word
3 **L**ast days bring apostasy
4 **D**iligently preach God's Word

TITUS

1 **S**ound doctrine silences error
2 **O**rder life to doctrine
3 **N**ever shun good deeds

PHILEMON

Verses

1-7   **L**etter of Philemon's love

8-14   **O**nesimus becomes a Christian

15-20   **V**indication requested for Onesimus

21-25   **E**xpectation cited by Paul

HEBREWS

1 **N**ature of God's Son
2 **E**xaltation after Christ's sacrifice
3 **W**orthy of man's obedience

4 **P**romise of believers' rest
5 **R**emember Christ like Melchizedek
6 **I**nheritance for persistent faith
7 **E**ternal priesthood of Melchizedek
8 **S**econd covenant supersedes first
9 **T**estimony of Christ's blood
10 **H**oliness through one sacrifice
11 **O**bedience of God's faithful
12 **O**bedience helped by discipline
13 **D**uties of the Christian

HERE COMES THE NEW PRIEST!

JAMES

1 **W**orking patience through trials
2 **O**bedience that accompanies faith
3 **R**estraining the unbridled tongue
4 **K**eeping calm in conflicts
5 **S**uffering and sick saints

FIRST PETER

1 **T**rials prove your faith
2 **R**espond like Christ's example
3 **I**nnocent conscience quiets foes
4 **A**ttitudes pleasing to God
5 **L**eaders to serve humbly

SECOND PETER

1 **A**dd virtue to faith
2 **D**eeds of false teachers
3 **D**iligence before the Lord's return

FIRST JOHN

SECOND JOHN

Verses
1-3 **L**ove for the lady
4-6 **A**dmonished to love others
7-11 **D**eception of the Antichrist
12-13 **Y**earning to pay a visit

THIRD JOHN

Verses
1-4 **G**reetings to brother Gaius
5-6 **A**ccept strangers and brethren
7-8 **I**nvest in God's work
9-10 **U**njust words of Diotrephes
11-14 **S**pecial thanks to Demetrius

JUDE

Verses

1-4   **J**ude warns against apostasy
5-7   **U**nbelief seen throughout history
8-19   **D**escription of false teachers
20-25 **E**xhortation to stay faithful

REVELATION

1 **P**atmos vision of John
2 **R**ebuke for four churches
3 **O**ther three churches rebuked
4 **P**icture of God's throne
5 **H**oly Lamb is worshiped
6 **E**ach seal is broken
7 **C**rowd coming from tribulation
8 **Y**oke of four trumpets

9 **A**byss releases more trumpets
10 **B**ook eaten by John
11 **O**pposition to two witnesses
12 **U**nrelenting opposition of dragon
13 **T**atoo of world ruler